BALLOON -A-HOAGIE

Written &
Illustrated by
O. R. Cabrera

Copyright © 2023 O. R. Cabrera

All rights reserved. No part of this publication may be reproduced, distributed, or transmitted in any form or by any means, including photocopying, recording, or other electronic or mechanical methods, without the prior written permission of the publisher, except in the case of brief quotations embodied in critical reviews and certain other noncommercial uses permitted by copyright law.

ISBN: 979-8-9883551-3-7 (Paperback)
ISBN: 979-8-9883551-2-0 (Hardcover)

Library of Congress Control Number: 2023908712

Any references to historical events, real people, or real places are used fictitiously. Names, characters, and places are products of the author's imagination.

Front cover image by Sarah Battistelli
Book design by Sarah Battistelli

Printed by Ricordo Publishing, LLC in the United States of America.

First printing edition 2023

To the late Angelo Randazzo, the brain behind Balloon-A-Hoagie and countless other intrepid (and as of yet untested) business ventures.

In a gray, sleepy Pennsylvania town, there were many, many hoagie shops.

One of these shops was owned by Angelo Montanari's parents, Antonietta and Sal.

They made
the **BEST**
hoagies
in town.

Customers formed a line that went out the door and snaked through the neighborhood. The hoagies were incredibly tasty, of course.

But many customers also came to see Angelo, who was renowned for being a charmingly quirky and helpful bambino.

The customers adored little Angelo, who busied himself sweeping dirt under the rug, scrubbing fingerprints off the glass with his bare hands and greeting customers with a loud and sharp, "Benvenuto!"

Benvenuto!

Benvenuto!

Benvenuto!

He would regularly draw pictures of his guinea pigs, Meatball and Gabagool, which he insisted be hung on the glass of the beverage cooler.

There were even two hoagies in the shop named after Angelo's guinea pigs (although his father insisted it was the other way around.)

Hoagies and guinea pigs. Guinea pigs and hoagies. These were the only concerns in little Angelo's head.

One day, almost out of nowhere, a great disruption arrived in town: one block over, a new restaurante opened **Prestini's Paninis.** They made sandwiches too!

Their sandwiches were not bigger or better or cheaper than Montanari's hoagies. Antonietta and Sal knew this.

Unfortunately, their customers were blinded by their billboards, news coverage... even their tik tok account!

All of Montanari's customers took one look at Prestini's colorful ads and glossy tri-fold fliers and they flocked over like racoons to trash.

When a shiny *Prestini's Paninis* flier showed up in the Montanari mailbox, Sal's face turned as red as a tomato.

He crumpled the waxy paper in his hand, stormed into his home, and slammed the door.

There was nothing to be done but to continue making the best hoagies they could. So, the next day and the next day and the next, that's exactly what Angelo's parents did. Antonietta and Sal made the best hoagies they ever had.

But the line that used to look like a snake winding up the sidewalk started to look more like a really short worm.

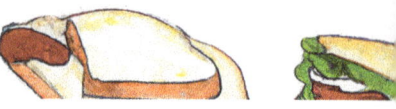

And then, there was no line at all.

The only loyal customer that remained was Mr. Grasso, who had a weird habit of saying "appreciate" between every other word, even when he wasn't thanking anyone for anything.

"Benvenuto, Mr. Grasso!"

"Appreciate! Appreciate! Appreciate!"

Beyond the hoagies sold to Mr. Grasso, business was not good. This made Angelo's papa sad despite Mr. Grasso's great appreciation.

Everything about his papa seemed to droop—his eyes, his shoulders, his hair. Angelo started to worry that Papa was powered by making and selling hoagies, like a Sandwich-Bot.

The thought scared him (although of course his father wasn't really powering down from a lack of hoagie-selling).

"Papa," Angelo said one night after dinner, "How can I help save our shop?"

Sal patted him on the shoulder and shook his head.

"These are grown-up problems with grown-up answers. You won't be of any help. Go do your homework. Maybe you can work in tech."

Angelo frowned. Work in tech? No way!
He was the Darling Bambino of Montanari's!
He wanted to make hoagies.

Defeated and upset, he went to his room
to discuss his problems with Meatball
and Gabagool.

They were no help.
They squeaked in sympathy, but gave him no
answers. How could he get the customers to
come back so his father would be happy again?

That night, Angelo could not sleep.
He was worried.
He was embarrassed.

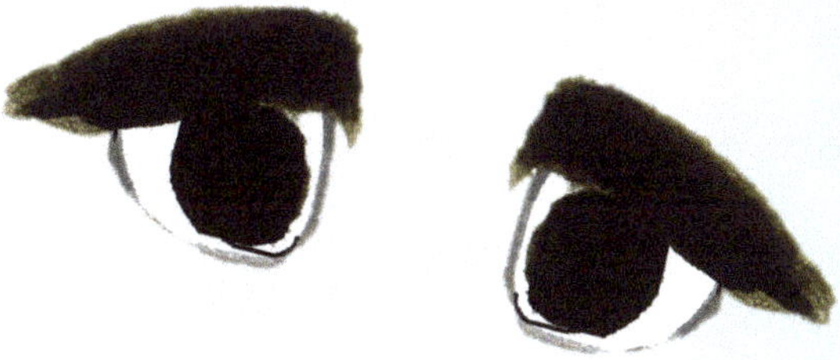

He tossed and turned.
When he closed his eyes,
all he saw were floating hoagies
and his dad's big, sad, droopy eyes.

He began to count sheep.

One...

    two...

        three...

            four...

                five...

Before long, the sheep started acting and looking a little bit funny.

Sheep number twelve was wearing a funny hat.

Number thirteen was the color of the rainbow.

Number fourteen was wearing high heels!

And finally, number fifteen handed Angelo a balloon...

Of course, the moment Angelo had drifted off to sleep, a loud noise stirred him. Meatball and Gabagool were squeaking intensely.

They must have heard the refrigerator door open.

Indeed, Angelo's father was poking through the fridge for a late-night, stress-induced slice of eggplant parmesan and the guinea pigs were now begging for one, too.

The racket had roused Angelo back into a loopy state between the real world and his dreams.

So, Angelo began to lazily count his sheep friends again ...

and there was number fifteen, with his balloon.

And that gave Angelo an idea.

Balloons. Hoagies. Balloon hoagies?
Hoagies in balloons? Hoagies with balloons?

Yes, that was it!
Balloon- a -Hoagie.

Angelo shot up.
There was no question he was fully awake now!

Buy a hoagie, get a balloon. It was brilliant!

Angelo was sure this would save Montanari's Hoagie Shop!

Nowhere else could you get a good hoagie with a balloon.

You couldn't even get a *bad* hoagie with a balloon.

Angelo quickly wrote his idea down so he'd remember in the morning.

Meatball and Gabagool were chomping at their boring pellets, sad that no good food had been brought to them despite their loud requests.

Angelo whispered to Meatball and Gabagool, "Don't worry, I'll share the money we bring in with Balloon-a-Hoagie. You won't be able to eat your celery fast enough," and then he turned over and went to sleep.

The next morning Angelo ran into the kitchen, where his mother and father were drinking coffee.

He threw his note from the night before on the table in front of them and waited.

Angelo's father glanced at the note without moving.

"Baffoon-a-Hoayie," he read.

"Ballon-a-Hoagie," Angelo corrected.

They stared at each other.

Angelo had a knot in his stomach from nerves. Would his papa laugh at him?

He suddenly thought that maybe Balloon-a-Hoagie wasn't a grown-up answer to this grown-up problem.

Angelo broke the silence and explained,

"Every time you sell a hoagie, a customer will get a balloon. This is how we will beat *Prestini's Paninis!* This will remind our friends that Montanari's Hoagie Shop is special!"

His mother and father looked at each other, confused. After a long pause, his mother said,

"Why not, *signorino?* We have nothing to lose. We launch the *Balloon-a-Hoagie Special* tomorrow."

Antonietta picked up the note and stuck it to the fridge with a tomato-shaped magnet.

The knot in Angelo's stomach untwisted and burst into butterflies. Angelo screamed with excitement. He ran to his room and scooped up Meatball and Gabagool, thanking them over and over for waking him with their greedy little squeals.

Meatball and Gabagool sat in his arms peacefully, happy that Montanari's would still be making enough money to feed them vegetables every day. Angelo could have sworn he saw a small smile on Meatball's chunky face and a wink from Gabagool.

The next day, Balloon-a-Hoagie was born.

His mother and father could barely keep up with the number of customers! Salami, peppers, shredded lettuce, tomatoes, pepperoni–

Antonietta and Sal threw all this goodness onto crusty hoagie rolls, (already drizzled with oil and vinegar), while Angelo tied balloons to the customers' wrists.

Soon red, blue, purple, green, yellow balloons bobbed down the sidewalks, floating from wrists, and filling the gray town with color.

And people with no balloons were curious, of course.

Where did the balloons come from? Was there a festival they didn't know about? A traveling circus?

"Montanari's Hoagie Shop!" they'd explain. "They're running a Balloon-a-Hoagie Special!"

That was the genius of Balloon-a-Hoagie. *You could SEE it*. Montanari's didn't need a billboard or flyers or a tik tok account. They now had walking commercials for their business in the form of balloons.

So the line at Montanari's Hoagie Shop grew a little longer each day.

Even the biggest billboards and the fastest flashing tik tok video couldn't save Prestini's Paninis.

They quit making paninis and instead, became a bakery. Prestini's Pies and Pastries Parlor.

The line to Montanari's Hoagie Shop once again snaked throughout the neighborhood.

Sal Montanari no longer looked like a deflated balloon.

Meatball and Gabagool each got nice and fat from all the carrots and bell peppers Angelo fed them.

And Angelo, the Bambino of Montanari's, once again busied himself sweeping dirt under the rug, scrubbing fingerprints off the glass with his bare hands and greeting customers with a loud and sharp,

"*Benvenuto!*"

CPSIA information can be obtained
at www.ICGtesting.com
Printed in the USA
BVHW010934220623
666251BV00007B/459